FELT FOREST FRIENDS

CREATE **20** ADORABLE WOODLAND ANIMALS!

Aimee Ray

becker&mayer!
BOOK PRODUCERS

CONTENTS

INTRODUCTION

Welcome to the cute world of *Felt Forest Friends*! This kit includes everything you will need to hand-sew ten adorable mini woodland creatures, plus extra instructions for ten more. You'll learn simple hand-sewing and embroidery stitches that you can use to embellish your little friends. You can easily put together a bit of felt, embroidery floss, and stuffing to create something special that's sure to make you smile. This kit includes materials to make the bear, beaver, hedgehog, acorn, raccoon, robin, tree, leaf, frog, and deer.

When you're finished sewing the creatures in this kit, you'll want to use what you've learned to go on to make more! Try customizing the patterns by using different colors or making up your own embroidered accents.

What to do with Felt Forest Friends:

- Stitch a little loop of floss or ribbon on the back, and you can hang one anywhere.
- Collect some branches and use them to make a baby mobile.
- String them onto ribbon to make a garland for a woodland-themed room or party.
- Tie one onto an extra-special gift package.
- Give one to a little kid to play with.
- Pin one to your shirt and wear it around.
- Hang one from your Christmas tree, or any large potted plant any time of year.
- Leave out the stuffing, leave the bottom open, and make finger puppets!
- Stick one on a magnet and put it on your fridge.
- Carry one in your bag or pocket and take pictures of him wherever you go, then post his adventures online!
- Give them away and make someone's day happier.

GETTING STARTED

Hand-sewing and embroidery are very easy to learn and require only a few basic tools and materials, most of which are provided with this kit. Read through this section before you start sewing your little creatures to get familiar with them.

Felt

Felt is a soft, durable fabric that is easy to work with since the edges don't fray when you cut them. To make your Felt Forest Friends, you'll just cut the pieces you need from the felt provided and sew them together.

Floss

Embroidery floss is used for hand embroidery and also makes a great thread for hand-sewing projects. This kit includes several colors of embroidery floss, which you will use both for embroidering faces and other embellishments onto your creatures, as well as sewing the felt parts together. Floss is made up of six individual threads twisted together. You can separate the threads and use just a few of them, or use all six. For sewing felt pieces together, you will separate out two of the six threads of floss to use. A good length of floss to cut is about twelve inches long.

Stuffing

Stuffing or fiberfill is what you will use to fill your Forest Friends and make them into little pillows. It can be pulled apart and pushed inside your felt shapes as you sew the fronts and backs together. A pencil or knitting needle can come in handy for stuffing small areas. Don't be too concerned with getting a lot of stuffing into tiny spaces like ears or feet—they will look just fine with a very small amount. For each creature you sew, you will stitch the front and back felt parts together around the edge leaving about an inch open at the end, then add your stuffing before closing up the hole. Don't cram in too much; you want just enough to make the sides puff out a bit, but not so much that the sewn seams are pulling apart. If it's easier, you can stuff bits of stuffing into small areas as you sew around the edges instead of waiting until the end.

Needle

A standard embroidery needle is also perfect for hand-sewing felt. It has a sharp point and a large eye that is easy to thread.

Scissors

Any type of sharp scissors will be fine for cutting out larger felt parts, but you will find a pair of small sewing or embroidery scissors will come in very handy for the smaller parts. They will make cutting around little ears and spots much easier.

Templates

Paper templates for each felt piece you will need are included in this kit. Simply place the template onto the felt, trace around it, and then cut the shape out of the felt. For lighter felt colors, you can use a fabric marker or a regular pencil to trace around the templates; for darker colors, you'll need white chalk or a chalk pencil. The instructions on the template pieces, as well as the instructions in this book, will tell you how many of each piece you will need for the creature you're making. Each creature has a front and a back body piece that match and will be sewn together around the edges, as well as a few extra pieces in different colors that will be stitched to the front piece. Once you've cut out all the felt pieces you need, you're ready to begin stitching.

Hand-Sewing Stitches

There are a few basic hand-sewing stitches you'll use to sew up your Forest Friends. They are easy to master, and before long, you'll be stitching up a whole menagerie!

Stab Stitch

The first thing you will do after you cut out the felt parts you need is to assemble the pieces of the front side of your creature. The stab stitch is used to sew a small piece of felt onto a larger piece, such as sewing the chest pieces onto the bear or raccoon body parts.

Separate two threads from a strand of floss matching the small piece of felt. Thread your needle and tie a knot in one end. Position the small felt piece on top of the larger one and bring the needle through both pieces from the back at A. Make a tiny stitch at B. Make your stitches ⅛ inch from the edge of the small piece, ⅛ inch apart, all around the edge to secure it down. When it's stitched in place, tie a knot in your thread at the back.

Whip Stitch

When you're finished embellishing the front of your creature, you're ready to sew the front and back parts together with the whip stitch. Separate two threads from a strand of floss that matches the felt and tie a knot in one end. Line up the front and back parts together with right sides facing out. Pin them if it makes it easier for you to hold them. At about ⅛ inch from the edge of the felt, push the needle through the top piece of felt from in between the two layers so that the knot is inside. Now wrap the thread around the outside edge of the two layers together, push the needle back up through both layers from the back at A, then over the edge again and back up from the back at B. Continue sewing the layers together with the whip stitch all around the edge, keeping your stitches small and about ⅛ inch apart.

Embroidery Stitches

You'll use a bit of hand embroidery to add faces and embellishments to your Forest Friends. These simple stitches will show you how. Since the pieces are small, trying to transfer a pattern for the embroidery would be difficult, but once you master these stitches, adding the embellishments will be easy as you refer to the illustrations to see which stitches to place where.

Straight Stitch

The most basic embroidery stitch is the straight stitch, and it can be used in a variety of ways. You will use several straight stitches in a group to make fur on some of the animals like the raccoon and bear and straight stitches in little V shapes on the owl and some of the faces. Use two or three of the six threads of floss for straight stitches. Simply knot your floss, pull the needle up through the felt at A, and push it down through again, ⅛ to ¼ inch away at B.

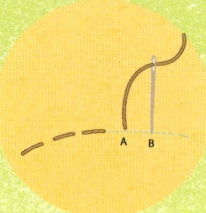

Back Stitch

The back stitch is used for making lines. You will use the back stitch to make lines on the hips of the squirrel and bunny, and veins on the leaf. Start with a small stitch in the opposite direction, from A to B. Bring your needle back up through the fabric at C, ahead of the first stitch and ending at A. Repeat to make a row of back stitches, working backward on the surface and inserting the needle at the end of each previous stitch.

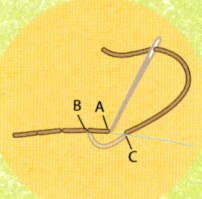

Satin Stitch

Satin stitches are used to make small, solid shapes such as eyes and noses. Use all six threads of floss when making satin stitches. Start by making a straight stitch from A to B. Make a second stitch right next to the first one from C to D. Always bring your needle up on one side and down on the other for best results. For an eye, start with a shorter stitch at the bottom, add two to three slightly longer stitches above it, then finish the circle with another shorter stitch at the top. The longest stitches for an eye should be between ⅛ and ¼ inch long. Use a tiny straight stitch in white over the top right of the circle to make a little shine on the eye. This tiny detail gives the eyes sparkle and character. To stitch a nose, start with a short stitch at the bottom and make three to four more stitches above it, each getting slightly longer as you go up, to form a triangle. The longest stitch in the nose should be about ¼ inch long.

Knots

You'll need to knot your floss before and after sewing to keep your stitches from coming loose. Here are three different knots to use for different purposes.

Roll Knot

This is one way to knot the end of your floss before you begin stitching. Thread one end of floss through the needle. Wrap the other end around the tip of your forefinger two or three times. Roll the floss up and over the end of your finger with your thumb, then pull the knot downward to tighten it. This creates a good-sized, strong knot that will catch easily at the back of the felt. This knot may take a little practice; if you have trouble, you can tie any regular knot at the end of your floss instead.

End Knot

When you finish an embroidery or stab stitch, you'll want to knot your floss at the back of your felt to hold the stitches in place. Simply slide your needle under the last stitch at the back, bring it back through the loop the thread creates, and pull the thread tightly to knot it.

Hidden Knot

This is the knot you'll use with the whip stitch when you sew the front and back of your creatures together. End your thread by making an end knot at the last whip stitch, just as you would at the back of your felt. Now slide the needle in between the two felt layers and bring it back up ½ inch or so away from the edge, pulling the knot just inside. Snip off the remaining thread close to the felt. Squeeze the felt just a bit and the end of the thread will be hidden inside. If you need to continue with whip stitches around the edge of your creature, simply start a new knot from in between the felt layers. Or, if you're done sewing it up, you're finished!

BUNNY FOREST FRIEND

Bunnies are the most common forest animal. They are shy but irresistible.

FINISHED SIZE: 3 INCHES LONG

Materials:

- One (2 x 3 inch) piece of gray felt
- One (1 x 2 inch) piece of cream felt
- Cream embroidery floss (DMC ECRU)
- White embroidery floss (DMC BLANC)
- Dark brown embroidery floss (DMC 898)
- Pink embroidery floss (DMC 352)
- Dark gray embroidery floss (DMC 3787)
- Gray embroidery floss (DMC 648)
- Stuffing

Instructions:

1. Using the enclosed bunny templates, trace the pieces onto the felt with a pen or fabric pencil. Cut two body pieces from gray felt and one ear, face, and two tail pieces from cream felt.

2. Sew the face and ear pieces to one of the gray body pieces using the stab stitch (see page 5) with two strands of cream floss. Line up the two tail pieces and sew around the edge using the whip stitch (see page 5) with two strands of cream floss, leaving a small hole. Stuff the tail lightly before closing it up.

3. Use the satin stitch (see page 6) with dark brown floss to embroider the eye, and then make a tiny white stitch on it. Use the satin stitch with pink floss to make the nose. Use the back stitch (see page 6) with dark gray floss for the hip line. Use Fig. 1 as a guide.

4. Line up the front and back pieces, and sew them together around the edge using the whip stitch with two strands of gray floss. Tuck the tail in between the body layers as you sew up the back end. Leave one inch open at the end and tuck some stuffing inside. Use just enough stuffing to make it pillowy, but not so much that the seams pull apart. Now stitch up the hole and tie a hidden knot (see page 7).

Fig. 1

SQUIRREL FOREST FRIEND

Squirrels love to play and dig. They bury lots of nuts but can't always remember where to find them!

FINISHED SIZE: 2 INCHES TALL

Materials:

- One (2 x 4 inch) piece of gray felt
- One (1 x 2 inch) piece of cream felt
- Cream embroidery floss (DMC ECRU)
- White embroidery floss (DMC BLANC)
- Dark brown embroidery floss (DMC 898)
- Dark gray embroidery floss (DMC 3787)
- Gray embroidery floss (DMC 648)
- Stuffing

Instructions:

1. Using the enclosed squirrel templates, trace the pieces onto the felt with a pen or fabric pencil. Cut two body pieces from gray felt, and cut one face and one tail piece from cream felt.

2. Sew the face and tail pieces to one of the gray body pieces using the stab stitch (see page 5) with two strands of cream floss.

3. Use the satin stitch (see page 6) with dark brown floss to embroider the eye and nose, then make a tiny white stitch on the eye. Use the back stitch (see page 6) with dark gray floss for the hip line and the satin stitch with dark gray floss for the ears. Use Fig. 2 as a guide.

4. Line up the front and back pieces, and sew them together around the edge using the whip stitch (see page 5) with two strands of gray floss. Leave one inch open at the end and tuck some stuffing inside. Use just enough stuffing to make it pillowy, but not so much that the seams pull apart. Now stitch up the hole and tie a hidden knot (see page 7).

Fig. 2

FOX FOREST FRIEND

This little fox is poised to leap and pounce!

FINISHED SIZE: 2.5 INCHES LONG

Materials:

- One (3 x 4 inch) piece of orange felt
- One (1 x 2 inch) piece of cream felt
- Cream embroidery floss (DMC ECRU)
- Dark brown embroidery floss (DMC 898)
- Dark orange embroidery floss (DMC 400)
- Orange embroidery floss (DMC 922)
- White embroidery floss (DMC BLANC)
- Stuffing

Instructions:

1. Using the enclosed fox templates, trace the pieces onto the felt with a pen or fabric pencil. Cut two body pieces from orange felt and one tail and one face piece from cream felt.

2. Position the cream felt pieces onto the front orange piece as shown in Fig. 3 and sew them in place using the stab stitch (see page 5) with two strands of cream floss.

3. Embroider the eye and nose using the satin stitch (see page 6) with dark brown floss. Add a tiny white stitch to the eye. Use the satin stitch with cream floss for the ear, and the straight stitch (see page 6) with dark orange floss onto front fox piece for the fur. Use Fig. 3 as a guide.

4. Line up the front and back pieces, and sew them together around the edge using the whip stitch (see page 5) with two strands of dark orange floss around the body and cream floss around the tail. Leave one inch open at the end and tuck a little stuffing inside. Use just enough stuffing to make it pillowy, but not so much that the seams pull apart. Now stitch up the hole and tie a hidden knot (see page 7).

Fig. 3

OWL FOREST FRIEND

Little owl is winking away his daytime sleepiness.

FINISHED SIZE: 2 INCHES TALL

Materials:

- **One (2 x 4 inch) piece of light brown felt**
- **One (1 x 2 inch) piece of cream felt**
- **One (1.5 x 1.5 inch) piece of gray felt**
- **One (0.5 x 0.5 inch) piece of dark brown felt**
- **Dark brown embroidery floss (DMC 898)**
- **Medium brown embroidery floss (DMC 434)**
- **Cream embroidery floss (DMC ECRU)**
- **White embroidery floss (DMC BLANC)**
- **Gray embroidery floss (DMC 648)**
- **Stuffing**

Instructions:

1. Using the enclosed owl templates, trace the pieces onto the felt with a pen or fabric pencil. Cut two body pieces from light brown felt; one chest piece from gray felt; one mask from cream felt; and one beak piece from dark brown felt.

2. Position the chest and mask pieces onto the front light brown piece as shown in Fig. 4, and sew them in place using the stab stitch (see page 5). Use two strands of gray floss for the chest and two strands of cream floss for the mask.

3. Use the satin stitch (see page 6) with dark brown floss to embroider one eye and straight stitch (see page 6) for the other eye. Add a tiny white stitch to the open eye. Make straight stitches in V shapes for the feathers on the chest using two strands of medium brown floss. Use Fig. 4 as a guide.

4. Line up the front and back pieces, and sew them together around the edge using the whip stitch (see page 5) with two strands of light brown floss. Leave one inch open at the end and tuck some stuffing inside. Use just enough stuffing to make it pillowy, but not so much that the seams pull apart. Now stitch up the hole and tie a hidden knot (see page 7).

Fig. 4

DEER FOREST FRIEND

Sweet and gentle baby fawns are camouflaged with spots to hide in the forest leaves.

FINISHED SIZE: 3 INCHES LONG

Materials:

- One (2 x 6 inch) piece of dark brown felt
- One (1 x 2 inch) piece of light brown felt
- Dark brown embroidery floss (DMC 898)
- Light brown embroidery floss (DMC 436)
- White embroidery floss (DMC BLANC)
- Black embroidery floss (DMC 310)
- Stuffing

Instructions:

1. Using the enclosed deer templates, trace the pieces onto the felt with a pen or fabric pencil. Cut two body pieces from dark brown felt; cut one face piece, one tail piece, and the three spots from light brown felt.

2. Position the spots, tail, and face pieces onto the front dark brown body piece as shown in Fig. 5, and sew them in place using the stab stitch (see page 5) with two strands of light brown floss.

3. Use the satin stitch (see page 6) with black floss to embroider the eye, then add a tiny white stitch to it. Use the satin stitch with dark brown floss to embroider the nose. Use Fig. 5 as a guide.

4. Line up the front and back pieces, and sew them together around the edge using the whip stitch (see page 5) with two strands of dark brown floss. Leave one inch open at the end and tuck some stuffing inside. Use just enough stuffing to make it pillowy, but not so much that the seams pull apart. Now stitch up the hole and tie a hidden knot (see page 7).

Fig. 5

ROBIN FOREST FRIEND

Robins are the first to announce spring has arrived.

FINISHED SIZE: 2.75 INCHES LONG

Materials:

- One (2 x 4 inch) piece of medium brown felt
- One (1 x 0.5 inch) piece of pink felt
- One (0.5 x 0.5 inch) piece of dark brown felt
- Dark brown embroidery floss (DMC 898)
- Medium brown embroidery floss (DMC 434)
- Pink embroidery floss (DMC 352)
- White embroidery floss (DMC BLANC)
- Stuffing

Instructions:

1. Using the enclosed robin templates, trace the pieces onto the felt with a pen or fabric pencil. Cut two body pieces and two wings from medium brown felt; one chest piece from pink felt; and one beak piece from dark brown felt.

2. Position the chest piece over a body piece as shown in Fig. 6, and sew it in place using the stab stitch (see page 5) with two strands of pink floss. Then stitch the beak piece in place using two strands of dark brown floss. Now position the wings in place on both front and back pieces. Make sure the front and back parts line up and that both wing parts are on the outside. Stitch the wings on using the stab stitch with two strands of medium brown floss.

3. Use the straight stitch (see page 6) with dark brown floss to embroider the eyes. Make straight stitches on the chest using two strands of medium brown floss. Use Fig. 6 as a guide.

4. Line up the front and back pieces of the body. Sew them together around the edge using the whip stitch (see page 5) with two strands of medium brown floss around the body and two strands of pink floss around the chest. Leave one inch open at the end and tuck some stuffing inside. Use just enough stuffing to make it pillowy, but not so much that the seams pull apart. Now stitch up the hole and tie a hidden knot (see page 7).

Fig. 6

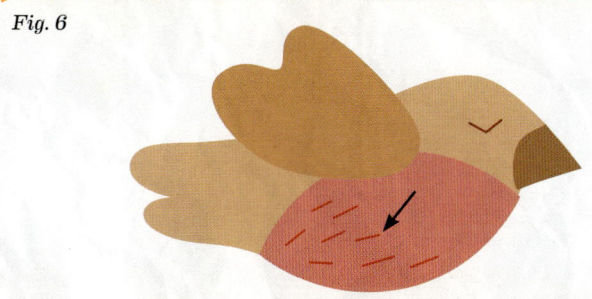

HEDGEHOG FOREST FRIEND

Hedgehogs make charming pets, but watch out for those spines!

FINISHED SIZE: 2.25 INCHES LONG

Materials:

- One (2 x 3 inch) piece of dark brown felt
- One (1 x 2 inch) piece of light brown felt
- Light brown embroidery floss (DMC 436)
- Dark brown embroidery floss (DMC 898)
- Medium brown embroidery floss (DMC 434)
- White embroidery floss (DMC BLANC)
- Stuffing

Instructions:

1. Using the enclosed hedgehog templates, trace the pieces onto the felt with a pen or fabric pencil. Cut two body pieces from dark brown felt and two head pieces from light brown felt.

2. Position each body piece over each head piece as shown in Fig. 7, and sew them in place using the stab stitch (see page 5) with two strands of dark brown floss. Make sure the front and back parts line up and that both body parts are on the outside.

3. Use the satin stitch (see page 6) with dark brown floss to embroider the eyes. Add a tiny white stitch to each eye. Use the satin stitch with dark brown floss to embroider the nose and the satin stitch with medium brown floss to embroider the ear. Make straight stitches (see page 6) for the spines on the body using two strands of medium brown floss. Use Fig. 7 as a guide.

4. Line up the front and back pieces of the body, and sew them together around the edge using the whip stitch (see page 5) with two strands of dark brown floss around the body and two strands of light brown floss around the head. Leave one inch open at the end and tuck some stuffing inside. Use just enough stuffing to make it pillowy, but not so much that the seams pull apart. Now stitch up the hole and tie a hidden knot (see page 7).

Fig. 7

RACCOON FOREST FRIEND

This raccoon is wearing a mask, but it doesn't hide his cuteness!

FINISHED SIZE: 2.5 INCHES TALL

Materials:

- One (1 x 1.5 inch) piece of light brown felt
- One (3 x 6 inch) piece of medium brown felt
- One (2 x 2 inch) piece of dark brown felt
- Dark brown embroidery floss (DMC 898)
- Medium brown embroidery floss (DMC 434)
- White embroidery floss (DMC BLANC)
- Black embroidery floss (DMC 310)
- Stuffing

Instructions:

1. Using the enclosed raccoon templates, trace the pieces onto the felt with a pen or fabric pencil. Cut two body pieces from medium brown felt; one chest piece from light brown felt; and mask and tail stripes from dark brown felt.

2. Position the dark brown and light brown felt pieces onto the front medium brown piece as shown in Fig. 8, and sew them in place using the stab stitch (see page 5) with two strands of medium brown floss for the chest and two strands of dark brown floss for the mask and tail pieces.

3. Use the satin stitch (see page 6) to embroider the eyes with black floss. Add a tiny white stitch to each eye. Use the satin stitch to embroider the nose with dark brown floss. Make straight stitches (see page 6) for the fur onto the chest using two strands of medium brown floss. Use Fig. 8 as a guide.

4. Line up the front and back pieces, and sew them together around the edge using the whip stitch (see page 5) with two strands of medium brown floss. Leave one inch open at the end and tuck some stuffing inside. Use just enough stuffing to make it pillowy, but not so much that the seams pull apart. Now stitch up the hole and tie a hidden knot (see page 7).

Fig. 8

BEAR FOREST FRIEND

Don't let his looks fool you—he's really quite ferocious!

FINISHED SIZE: 2.5 INCHES TALL

Materials:

- One (3 x 5 inch) piece of dark brown felt
- One (2 x 2 inch) piece of medium brown felt
- Dark brown embroidery floss (DMC 898)
- Medium brown embroidery floss (DMC 434)
- White embroidery floss (DMC BLANC)
- Black embroidery floss (DMC 310)
- Stuffing

Instructions:

1. Using the enclosed bear templates, trace the pieces onto the felt with a pen or fabric pencil. Cut two body pieces from dark brown felt; cut one chest piece and one face piece from medium brown felt.

2. Position the chest and face pieces onto the front dark brown piece as shown in Fig. 9, and sew them in place using the stab stitch (see page 5) with two strands of medium brown floss.

3. Use the satin stitch (see page 6) with black floss to embroider the eyes. Add a tiny white stitch to each eye. Use the satin stitch with dark brown floss to embroider the nose, and add a short straight stitch underneath. Make straight stitches (see page 6) for the fur on the chest using two strands of dark brown floss. Use Fig. 9 as a guide.

4. Line up the front and back pieces, and sew them together around the edge using the whip stitch (see page 5) with two strands of dark brown floss. Leave one inch open at the end and tuck some stuffing inside. Use just enough stuffing to make it pillowy, but not so much that the seams pull apart. Now stitch up the hole and tie a hidden knot (see page 7).

Fig. 9

BUTTERFLY FOREST FRIEND

Butterflies are gentle and beautiful, like living flowers.

FINISHED SIZE: 1.75 INCHES LONG

Materials:

- One (2 x 2 inch) piece of black felt
- One (1 x 2 inch) piece of orange felt
- One (1 x 2 inch) piece of white felt
- Orange embroidery floss (DMC 922)
- White embroidery floss (DMC BLANC)
- Black embroidery floss (DMC 310)
- Stuffing

Instructions:

1. Using the enclosed butterfly templates, trace the pieces onto the felt with a pen or fabric pencil. Cut two body pieces from white felt; two wing pieces from black felt; and one of each stripe from orange felt.

2. Sew the stripes to one of the black wing pieces using the stab stitch (see page 5) with two strands of orange floss.

3. Use the straight stitch (see page 6) with black floss to embroider the eye and mouth. Sew the front and back body pieces together with a bit of stuffing inside. Use the back stitch (see page 6) with two strands of black floss to stitch the lines on the orange sections of the wings. Make white spots on the edges of the wings with the satin stitch (see page 6). Use Fig. 10 as a guide.

4. Line up the front and back wing pieces, and sew them together around the edge using the whip stitch (see page 5) with two strands of black floss. Tuck the body in between the wing layers at the bottom as you sew it up and tie a hidden knot (see page 7).

Fig. 10

BEE FOREST FRIEND

Busy, buzzy bumblebees are cute and fuzzy, but don't get too close!

FINISHED SIZE: 1.5 INCHES LONG

Materials:

- One (1 x 2 inch) piece of yellow felt
- One (1 x 1 inch) piece of black felt
- One (1 x 2 inch) piece of white felt
- Yellow embroidery floss (DMC 3821)
- White embroidery floss (DMC BLANC)
- Black embroidery floss (DMC 310)
- Light gray embroidery floss (DMC 648)
- Stuffing

Instructions:

1. Using the enclosed bee templates, trace the pieces onto the felt with a pen or fabric pencil. Cut two body pieces from yellow felt; two wing pieces from white felt; and one of each stripe from black felt.

2. Sew the stripes to one of the yellow body pieces using the stab stitch (see page 5) with two strands of black floss.

3. Use the straight stitch (see page 6) with white floss to embroider the eye and mouth. Use the back stitch (see page 6) with two strands of light gray floss to stitch the lines on the wings. Use Fig. 11 as a guide. Sew the front and back wing pieces together with two strands of white floss using the whip stitch (see page 5).

4. Line up the front and back pieces and sew them together around the edge using the whip stitch with two strands of black floss around the black parts and yellow floss around the yellow parts. Tuck the wings in between the body layers at the top as you sew it up. Leave one inch open at the end and tuck some stuffing inside. Use just enough stuffing to make it pillowy, but not so much that the seams pull apart. Now stitch up the hole and tie a hidden knot (see page 7).

Fig. 11

BEAVER FOREST FRIEND

NO. 12

Beavers are the woodland's hardest workers.

FINISHED SIZE: 2.5 INCHES TALL

Materials:

- One (1 x 2 inch) piece of dark brown felt
- One (2 x 6 inch) piece of medium brown felt
- One (1 x 2 inch) piece of light brown felt
- Light brown embroidery floss (DMC 436)
- Dark brown embroidery floss (DMC 898)
- Medium brown embroidery floss (DMC 434)
- White embroidery floss (DMC BLANC)
- Stuffing

Instructions:

1. Using the enclosed beaver templates, trace the pieces onto the felt with a pen or fabric pencil. Cut two body pieces from medium brown felt; one chest piece from light brown felt; and two tail pieces from dark brown felt.

2. Position the chest piece onto the front medium brown piece as shown in Fig. 12, and sew it in place using the stab stitch (see page 5) with two strands of light brown floss.

3. Use the satin stitch (see page 6) with dark brown floss to embroider the eyes. Add a tiny white stitch to each eye. Use the satin stitch with dark brown floss to embroider the nose, and add two short straight stitches underneath for the mouth. Use the satin stitch in white floss to make teeth under the mouth, then stitch one more dark brown straight stitch in the center of them. Make straight stitches (see page 6) with two strands of medium brown floss for the fur on the chest. Make crisscrossing straight stitches on the tail with two strands of medium brown floss. Use Fig. 12 as a guide.

4. Line up the front and back pieces of the tail, and sew them together around the edge using the whip stitch (see page 5) with two strands of dark brown floss. Line up the front and back pieces of the body, and sew them together around the edge using the whip stitch with two strands of medium brown floss. Tuck the flat end of the tail in between the two body pieces at the right side as you stitch them together. Leave one inch open at the end and tuck some stuffing inside. Use just enough stuffing to make it pillowy, but not so much that the seams pull apart. Now stitch up the hole and tie a hidden knot (see page 7).

Fig. 12

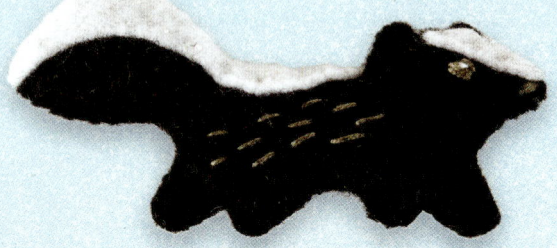

NO. 13 SKUNK FOREST FRIEND

Skunks may be cute, but they have a smelly little secret.

FINISHED SIZE: 3.25 INCHES LONG

Materials:

- One (2 x 3 inch) piece of black felt
- One (1 x 2 inch) piece of white felt
- White embroidery floss (DMC BLANC)
- Black embroidery floss (DMC 310)
- Dark gray embroidery floss (DMC 3787)
- Stuffing

Instructions:

1. Using the enclosed skunk templates, trace the pieces onto the felt with a pen or fabric pencil. Cut two body pieces from black felt and one of each stripe from white felt.

2. Sew the stripes to one of the black body pieces using the stab stitch (see page 5) with two strands of white floss.

3. Use the straight stitch (see page 6) with dark gray floss to embroider the fur lines. Use the satin stitch (see page 6) with dark gray floss to embroider the eye and nose. Add a tiny white stitch to the eye. Use Fig. 13 as a guide.

4. Line up the front and back body pieces, and sew them together around the edge using the whip stitch (see page 5) with two strands of black floss at the black parts and white floss around the stripes. Leave one inch open at the end and tuck some stuffing inside. Use just enough stuffing to make it pillowy, but not so much that the seams pull apart. Now stitch up the hole and tie a hidden knot (see page 7).

Fig. 13

 # FROG FOREST FRIEND

Frogs are happy creatures, content both on land and in the water.

FINISHED SIZE: 2 INCHES TALL

Materials:

- One (1 x 2 inch) piece of light green felt
- One (2 x 2 inch) piece of dark green felt
- White embroidery floss (DMC BLANC)
- Dark brown embroidery floss (DMC 898)
- Light green embroidery floss (DMC 472)
- Dark green embroidery floss (DMC 469)
- Stuffing

Instructions:

1. Using the enclosed frog templates, trace the pieces onto the felt with a pen or fabric pencil. Cut two body pieces from dark green felt; cut one chest piece and the four spots from light green felt.

2. Sew the chest piece and spots to one of the dark green body pieces using the stab stitch (see page 5) with two strands of light green floss.

3. Use the satin stitch (see page 6) with dark brown floss to embroider the eye. Add a tiny white stitch to the eye. Use the back stitch (see page 6) with dark brown floss to make the mouth. Use Fig. 14 as a guide.

4. Line up the front and back pieces, and sew them together around the edge using the whip stitch (see page 5) with two strands of dark green floss around the body and light green floss around the chest. Leave one inch open at the end and tuck some stuffing inside. Use just enough stuffing to make it pillowy, but not so much that the seams pull apart. Now stitch up the hole and tie a hidden knot (see page 7).

Fig. 14

SNAIL FOREST FRIEND

Snails carry their houses on their backs, but it makes them take life slowly and patiently.

FINISHED SIZE: 1.75 INCHES LONG

Materials:

- One (1.5 x 2 inch) piece of pink felt
- One (1 x 3 inch) piece of cream felt
- Pink embroidery floss (DMC BLANC)
- Cream embroidery floss (DMC ECRU)
- Dark gray embroidery floss (DMC 3787)
- Stuffing

Instructions:

1. Using the enclosed snail templates, trace the pieces onto the felt with a pen or fabric pencil. Cut two body pieces and the shell curl from cream felt; cut two shell pieces from pink felt.

2. Sew the curl to one of the pink shell pieces using the stab stitch (see page 5) with two strands of cream floss.

3. Use the straight stitch (see page 6) with dark gray floss to embroider the eye. Use Fig. 15 as a guide.

4. Line up the front and back body pieces, and sew them together around the edge using the whip stitch (see page 5) with two strands of cream floss. Leave one inch open at the end and tuck some stuffing inside before you close it up. Line up the front and back shell pieces, and sew them together around the edge using the whip stitch with two strands of pink floss. Tuck some stuffing inside. Use just enough stuffing to make it pillowy, but not so much that the seams pull apart. Sew the body part in between the shell layers as you sew up the bottom, then tie a hidden knot (see page 7).

Fig. 15

TREE FOREST FRIEND

You will be stitching a forest of these happy little trees!

FINISHED SIZE: 3 INCHES TALL

Materials:

- One (1 x 2 inch) piece of light green felt
- One (2 x 3 inch) piece of dark green felt
- One (1 x 0.5 inch) piece of dark brown felt
- Dark brown embroidery floss (DMC 898)
- Light green embroidery floss (DMC 472)
- Dark green embroidery floss (DMC 469)
- Stuffing

Instructions:

1. Using the enclosed tree templates, trace the pieces onto the felt with a pen or fabric pencil. Cut two body pieces from dark green felt; one center piece from light green felt; and two trunk pieces from dark brown felt.

2. Sew the center piece to one of the dark green body pieces using the stab stitch (see page 5) with two strands of light green floss. Sew the two trunk pieces together using the whip stitch (see page 5) with dark brown floss. Tuck a little stuffing inside.

3. Use the back stitch (see page 6) with dark brown floss to make the mouth and eyes. Make straight stitches (see page 6) in dark green all over the center piece around the face. Use Fig. 16 as a guide.

4. Line up the front and back pieces, and sew them together around the edge using the whip stitch with two strands of dark green floss. Tuck the trunk in between the layers at the bottom as you sew it up. Leave one inch open at the end and tuck some stuffing inside. Use just enough stuffing to make it pillowy, but not so much that the seams pull apart. Now stitch up the hole and tie a hidden knot (see page 7).

Fig. 16

ACORN FOREST FRIEND

Acorns are so much fun to collect, you'll want to sew a whole family of them in different colors!

FINISHED SIZE: 2 INCHES TALL

Materials:

- One (1 x 3 inch) piece of medium brown felt
- One (1 x 3 inch) piece of light brown felt
- Light brown embroidery floss (DMC 436)
- Dark brown embroidery floss (DMC 898)
- Medium brown embroidery floss (DMC 434)
- Pink embroidery floss (DMC 352)
- Stuffing

Instructions:

1. Using the enclosed acorn templates, trace the pieces onto the felt with a pen or fabric pencil. Cut two bottom pieces from light brown felt and two top pieces from medium brown felt.

2. Position each top piece over each bottom piece as shown in Fig. 17 and sew them in place using the stab stitch (see page 5) with two strands of medium brown floss. Make sure the front and back parts line up and that both top pieces are on the outside.

3. Use the straight stitch (see page 6) with dark brown floss to embroider the eyes and mouth on the bottom. Use crisscrossing straight stitches for the lines on the top. Use the satin stitch (see page 6) with pink floss to make cheeks under the eyes. Use Fig. 17 as a guide.

4. Line up the front and back pieces, and sew them together around the edge using the whip stitch (see page 5) with two strands of medium brown floss around the top and two strands of light brown floss around the bottom. Leave one inch open at the end and tuck some stuffing inside. Use just enough stuffing to make it pillowy, but not so much that the seams pull apart. Now stitch up the hole and tie a hidden knot (see page 7).

Fig. 17

MUSHROOM FOREST FRIEND

This happy little mushroom is a great companion for your woodland menagerie.

FINISHED SIZE: 1.75 INCHES TALL

Materials:

- One (2 x 2 inch) piece of pink felt
- One (1 x 2 inch) piece of white felt
- White embroidery floss (DMC BLANC)
- Dark brown embroidery floss (DMC 898)
- Pink embroidery floss (DMC 352)
- Stuffing

Instructions:

1. Using the enclosed mushroom templates, trace the pieces onto the felt with a pen or fabric pencil. Cut two bottom pieces and three spots from white felt; cut two top pieces from pink felt.

2. Sew the spots to one of the pink top pieces using the slab stitch (see page 5). Position each top piece over each bottom piece as shown in Fig. 18, and sew them in place using the stab stitch with two strands of pink floss. Make sure the front and back parts line up and that both top pieces are on the outside.

3. Use the satin stitch (see page 6) with dark brown floss to embroider the eyes, and the satin stitch with pink floss to make the cheeks. Add a tiny white stitch to each eye. Use the straight stitch (see page 6) with dark brown floss to make the mouth. Use Fig. 18 as a guide.

4. Line up the front and back pieces, and sew them together around the edge using the whip stitch (see page 5) with two strands of pink floss around the top and two strands of white floss around the bottom. Leave one inch open at the end and tuck some stuffing inside. Use just enough stuffing to make it pillowy, but not so much that the seams pull apart. Now stitch up the hole and tie a hidden knot (see page 7).

Fig. 18

PINECONE FOREST FRIEND

Pinecones have lots of character, especially this happy little one.

FINISHED SIZE: 2.5 INCHES TALL

Materials:

- One (2 x 5 inch) piece of medium brown felt
- Dark brown embroidery floss (DMC 898)
- Medium brown embroidery floss (DMC 434)
- White embroidery floss (DMC BLANC)
- Stuffing

Instructions:

1. Using the enclosed pinecone templates, trace the pieces onto the felt with a pen or fabric pencil. Cut all parts from medium brown felt.

2. Position the front, scalloped pieces over each other, overlapping them. Start with the bottom piece, layer the piece with two scallops on top of it, then both three scallop pieces, then the stem piece at the top. Make sure the front layered part lines up with the back part of the pinecone. Sew the front pieces in place using a stab stitch (see page 5) at the top corner between each scallop with two strands of medium brown floss.

3. Use the straight stitch (see page 6) with dark brown floss to embroider the mouth. Use the satin stitch (see page 6) with dark brown floss to embroider the eyes. Add a tiny white stitch to each eye. Use Fig. 19 as a guide.

4. Line up the front and back pieces of the pinecone, and sew them together around the edge using the whip stitch (see page 5) with two strands of medium brown floss. Leave one inch open at the end and tuck some stuffing inside. Use just enough stuffing to make it pillowy, but not so much that the seams pull apart. Now stitch up the hole and tie a hidden knot (see page 7).

Fig. 19

LEAF FOREST FRIEND

Leaves are everywhere in the forest, and each one is unique.

FINISHED SIZE: 2 INCHES TALL

Materials:

- One (2 x 2 inch) piece of light green felt
- White embroidery floss (DMC BLANC)
- Dark brown embroidery floss (DMC 898)
- Light green embroidery floss (DMC 472)
- Dark green embroidery floss (DMC 469)
- Stuffing

Instructions:

1. Using the enclosed leaf templates, trace the pieces onto the felt with a pen or fabric pencil. Cut two body pieces from light green felt.

2. Use the satin stitch (see page 6) with dark brown floss to embroider the eyes. Add a tiny white stitch to each eye. Use the back stitch (see page 6) with dark brown floss to make the mouth. Use the back stitch with dark green floss to make the leaf veins. Use Fig. 20 as a guide.

3. Line up the front and back pieces, and sew them together around the edge using the whip stitch (see page 5) with two strands of light green floss. Leave one inch open at the end and tuck some stuffing inside. Use just enough stuffing to make it pillowy, but not so much that the seams pull apart. Now stitch up the hole and tie a hidden knot (see page 7).

Fig. 20

becker&mayer!
BOOK PRODUCERS

11120 NE 33rd Pl #101, Bellevue, WA 98004
www.beckermayer.com

Editor: Dana Youlin
Designer: Sam Dawson
Production Coordinators: Cindy Curren and Jen Matasich
Photographer: Joe Lambert

83450-900-469-2

This book is part of the *Felt Forest Friends* kit
and is not to be sold separately.

Manufactured in Shenzhen, China

Image Credits: Box: green leaves seamless pattern © Zubada/Shutterstock; vector
tree rings background and saw cut tree trunk © microvector/Shutterstock. Book
cover: green leaves seamless pattern © Zubada/Shutterstock; slice of wood timber
natural background © Maxim Tupikov/Shutterstock. Book interior: page 1:
green leaves seamless pattern © Zubada/Shutterstock. Page 2: vector tree rings
background and saw cut tree trunk © microvector/Shutterstock. Used throughout:
slice of wood timber natural background © Maxim Tupikov/Shutterstock; white
crumpled paper texture for background © aopsan/Shutterstock

Project #16480